Street Therapy

A Dose of Reality

by

Olivia J. Hernandez

Street Therapy

Printed In United States of America

DEDICATION

To my husband Joseluis and my two boys Davis and Lucius, the joy and purpose in my every day. To my sister, DeAnna, whose love has been a steady light. To my dear friend Jen, for planting the seed of this cover idea nearly twenty years ago. To the friends who walked beside me when the road was heavy. And most of all, to God who never left my side and kept knocking until I let Him in.

PREFACE

This book is my testimony.

It is not written by any professional or therapist, but from the heart of a woman who was born addicted to heroin, witnessed her mother's murder, endured foster care and adoption, and faced many other curveballs life threw her way.

I fought through addiction. I survived mental, emotional, and other forms of abuse, and each time when life tried to break me, I emerged stronger. My past shaped me, but it never defined my worth.

I was a single mother for eighteen years. Today, I am married and blessed with two boys. My healing began in California in 2004 and came full circle in Texas in 2017. Through every struggle, I discovered a strength I didn't know I had – a strength that kept me going and I never gave up.

What you'll find in these pages are lessons, reflections, and truths. Some are my own, and some have been borrowed from others. My hope is that they speak to you especially if you've ever felt forgotten, broken, or stuck. Healing is possible, but it begins with facing your pain and choosing to rise above it.

I might not have all the answers, but I know recovery is real. Therapy, support groups, books, and simply observing life have all helped shape me into the woman I am today: a woman fighting daily for her sobriety, peace, freedom and navigating demanding society.

This is my truth. I have lived it, survived it, and continue to overcome it. I am a winner, not because life became easy, but because I refuse to stop fighting.

May these words inspire you to begin your own journey of healing and freedom.

TABLE OF CONTENTS

SECTION 1

Recovery and Self-discovery

Recovery and self-discovery is the work of choosing yourself again. It is the decision to step into sobriety, confront anger without letting it define you, and rebuild through intentional self-care. Starting over becomes an act of strength, not failure. Each step forward shapes healing into something meaningful, grounded, and lasting.

Healing starts with courage and ends with purpose.

The Codependent One

A personal reflection on codependency and self-reliance

Understanding codependency: A personal perspective

To me, codependency isn't just a clinical term, it's a lived reality. It is the inability or unwillingness to stand alone, an unhealthy reliance on others for emotional support, validation, or even basic needs. Codependency convinces people they're incapable of navigating life independently, so they cling to others to fill the gaps they're too afraid to face on their own.

Recognizing codependent behavior

Codependency takes many forms, but at its core, it is dependency. It can look like relying on others for shelter, financial support, or emotional stability while avoiding personal responsibility and growth. Acknowledging these patterns is painful but necessary because change begins with truth.

The impact on relationships and family

Many people stay in codependent roles out of fear or for family. Some parents justify staying stuck "for the sake of a child," but what happens when that child grows up, starts working, and becomes responsible, while the parent remains dependent? This imbalance reveals the heart of codependency: fear of independence and a lack of self-belief.

Financial control and burden

Codependency can also appear as trying to control resources that aren't yours dictating how others should support you. This only deepens the cycle and places a heavy burden on relationships. No one is obligated to carry someone else's responsibilities forever.

Breaking the cycle

Independence isn't only about empowering, it's crucial in so many ways. Codependency feeds stereotypes, weakens families, and robs individuals of their true potential. But the cycle can be broken. Across the globe, seminars, workshops, and support groups exist to help build self-reliance and confidence. It's never too late to learn, to grow, and to reclaim control of your life.

Learning from role models

Sometimes our greatest teachers are those closest to us even our children. If your daughter is working hard, standing tall, and showing responsibility, let her strength inspire you. There is no shame in learning from those who walk ahead of you.

A wake-up call

Codependency is a trap that can leave you isolated if ignored. Breaking free requires honesty, courage, and a willingness to change. The journey may seem difficult, but the rewards like independence, dignity, and healthier relationships make it worthwhile.

Embracing Control and Change

Finding stability in an unpredictable world

The humor in seeking control

In today's fast-paced, chaotic world, the idea of control can feel almost comical. We chase it, hoping for stability amidst constant change, yet life rarely unfolds according to plan. Trying to orchestrate every detail can feel futile, but that realization can free us. Embracing humor in our attempts to control the uncontrollable changes moods and helps us move through uncertainty with resilience.

The virtue of patience

Patience is an acquired taste, one that many resist in a world of instant gratification. Yet, it is patience that steadies us when progress feels slow. By cultivating patience, we learn to trust the process, to breathe through setbacks, and to appreciate every stage of our journey.

Focusing on good-hearted qualities

While external circumstances shift, our good-hearted traits kindness, empathy, and integrity remain unshakable anchors. Centering ourselves on these qualities builds an inner foundation – a foundation so strong that no storm can shake it. Our character becomes our compass, guiding us with clarity and purpose.

The importance of self-reflection and adaptability

It's easy to become consumed with the image we project outwardly, forgetting that the exterior is just a costume. Real growth comes from within through self-reflection, self-honesty, and a willingness to adapt. Change, far from being a threat, is a powerful opportunity for reinvention and renewal.

Welcoming change

In truth, change hasn't hurt us, it has shaped us. By releasing rigid control, embracing patience, leaning into our good-hearted nature, and welcoming change, we create the resilience needed to thrive. Each moment of growth brings us closer to becoming the strongest, most authentic version of ourselves.

Self-Care

Self-care is not selfish, it's survival

The prerequisite

Taking care of yourself is the foremost condition for loving and supporting others. Your ambition and drive must be so strong that they should be enough to push you forward. You just need to let go of the unnecessary burdens weighing you down, they're not yours to carry.

No place for negativity

Declutter your mind of toxic thoughts. Spend time alone when needed, reflecting on who you are and how you want to show up in the world. The habits you create will influence everyone around you. Be intentional about becoming a source of encouragement and light. When you see your reflection, honor your inner beauty, everything else will follow.

Own the setback, don't live in it

Setbacks are lessons, not life sentences. Own them, learn from them, and move forward. Don't let the idea of failure define you. When you start something new, commit fully, that's how you grow stronger and more capable. Distance yourself from those who drain you with empty words and hidden unhappiness. Stay authentic. Believing in yourself makes every challenge easier to conquer.

Starting Over: Embracing Freedom and the Promise of a Brighter Future

Letting go of the past and choosing happiness

Reclaiming your life after letting go

There comes a time when the weight of the past becomes too heavy to carry. Mistakes, painful memories, toxic relationships, they can all anchor you to places you've outgrown. Starting over isn't just about moving on; it's about reclaiming your courage and celebrating the strength it took to break free.

Breaking free from the chains of the past

Past pressures have a way of trying to drag you back into familiar cycles of unrest and pain. But peace lives on the other side of letting go. True freedom is not only physical, but also emotional and mental. It's the conscious choice to stop revisiting wounds that no longer deserve your presence.

Finding joy in release

Letting go creates space for joy, healing, and growth. Freedom isn't just the absence of hurt; it's the presence of possibility. Each day is a fresh chance to nurture self-love, explore new perspectives, and step into a brighter future without dragging yesterday along.

Owning your power

Starting over teaches you this: you are responsible for your happiness. If you step back into pain, you choose it. Fear of the unknown can trick you into clinging to what's harmful, but the life you want waits outside your comfort zone. Happiness may feel strange now, but in reality, it waits to be embraced.

Embracing a brighter future

The promise of tomorrow is real; it belongs to you if you claim it. Refuse to be held hostage by the past. Celebrate your release. Guard your peace. Embrace joy. Step boldly into the light and let your new freedom become the foundation of a life filled with hope, peace, and possibility.

- Celebrate the strength it took to walk away.
- Guard your peace and protect your growth.
- Let go of fear and welcome joy.
- Look forward, your future is brighter than your past.

Turning Anger into Determination

A reflection on self-worth and societal expectations

Embracing my journey

We all face moments of frustration when life doesn't align with our dreams. I've felt the sting of not being where I wanted to be. But instead of letting anger consume me, I use it as fuel. Every setback becomes a steppingstone, every disappointment a lesson. My anger sharpens into determination, reminding me: my time will come. Fear has no room in my heart when patience and persistence are guiding me forward.

Rejecting shallow standards

Society tries to measure worth in glitter, gold, and fame. If you don't fit that mold, you're told you don't measure up. But I refuse to buy into that lie. My value isn't defined by wealth or status, it's defined by authenticity, strength, and resilience. I will not let shallow standards dictate my worth.

Staying true to myself

I know who I am and what I stand for. My success won't be measured by someone else's scoreboard but by my own growth, dignity, and purpose. No one can diminish me for living authentically and choosing integrity over image.

Moving forward with confidence

The path won't always be easy, but I am determined. My anger doesn't weaken me, it strengthens me. I'll keep moving forward, chasing my goals on my own terms. My fire is not for destruction, but for creation.

Overcoming a Challenging Reality

A self-help reflection on identity and being genuine

Understanding discomfort and disconnection

It's not uncommon to wake each morning with a sense of unease, feeling disconnected from the person you've become. Often, this happens when outside expectations and societal norms shape us more than our own values and aspirations. The reflection in the mirror may look familiar, but deep down it doesn't feel like *you.*

The impact of external influences

In structured environments like the corporate world, routines and unspoken rules can feel suffocating at times. While society promotes "acceptable" standards and habits, those very standards can isolate you, creating a disconnect between who you are, and who you're expected to be.

Embracing authenticity

Freedom begins when you reject imposed narratives and embrace authenticity. Living as your true self, valued, confident, and unapologetic isn't just a dream, it's a right. The journey may feel distant while obligations and routines weigh heavily, but authenticity always begins with small, and informed steps.

Strategies for navigating challenges

- Reflect on your core values and personal goals.
- Surround yourself with people and environments that encourage authenticity.
- Set firm boundaries with expectations that don't align with your truth.
- Practice self-compassion as you grow into the fullest version of yourself.

The journey of personal authenticity

Authenticity isn't a finish line, it's a practice. By honoring your true self each day, you move closer to freedom, peace, and self-acceptance, even while meeting the demands of everyday life.

Made Stronger

How life's struggles shape resilience and character

Embracing adversity as fuel for growth

The struggles I've faced in my life may look like bad luck to others, but for me, they've been my guiding path. Each setback taught me to choose, stay down and be defeated, or rise, shake off the dust, and keep moving forward head on. My attitude determines whether the road feels heavy or light.

Transforming setbacks into opportunities

Every challenge is a lesson in disguise. Instead of obstacles, I see steppingstones, pushing me to think differently, build new strategies, and grow stronger with each trial. Hardship doesn't shrink me; it stretches me.

The power of attitude in overcoming hardship

Mindset changes everything. If I meet challenges with defeat, they crush me. But with determination and optimism, they shape me, refine me, and even give me joy. Struggles become teachers, not tormentors.

Faith and persistence the steamroller mindset

I don't fear bumps in the road anymore. With faith and persistence, I roll right over them. Like a steamroller, I flatten obstacles into a smoother path, keeping my eyes fixed on the prize. Nothing can stop a spirit fueled by resilience and belief.

Strength born from struggle

Hardship has become the hammer that forged my strength. Every trial has made me wiser, tougher, and more resilient. My struggles don't define me, they guide me, build me, and make me a stronger version of myself.

SECTION 2

Parenting and Growth Through Setbacks

Parenting and growth through setbacks is a journey shaped by connection, resilience, and grace. The bond between parent and child is strengthened not by flawless moments, but by consistency, honesty, and care. Choosing presence over perfection allows love to lead, even in difficult seasons. Honoring an absent parent with dignity becomes an act of healing rather than bitterness, creating space for understanding and growth.

Parenthood isn't about being perfect, it's about showing up with love.

Love Shivers

A personal reflection on the meaning and power of love

The complexity of expressing love

The word *love* carries immense weight. It's spoken often in conversations, songs, and stories, yet its true meaning can get lost in repetition. For some, love stirs deep emotions, both tender and painful. For me, the word itself has always sent shivers down my spine.

Growing up, I rarely heard it spoken aloud. Love wasn't said, it was shown in gestures, in fleeting moments of care. Because of this, the word felt heavy, foreign like it belonged to another language or another world. I often wondered if people simply had other priorities, or if, like me, they found the word daunting.

The emotional impact of "love"

Even now, the word brings a mix of fear and vulnerability. Saying "I love you" can feel risky, as if it opens the door to rejection or disappointment. Perhaps that's why it's so powerful, because to speak it sincerely is an act of courage.

Discovering true love through motherhood

Despite my discomfort, there is one place where love flows freely: with my sons. Through motherhood, I discovered love's truest meaning. It is sacrifice and care, laughter and protection, presence and patience. In this bond, love feels real, genuine, and safe.

My realization

Love may still bring shivers, but I've learned that it's more than a word. It's a force. It heals, binds, and strengthens. Love is not defined by how often it's spoken, but by how deeply it's lived.

The Gift of Love: A Parent's Reflection

Understanding the heartfelt legacy passed from parent to child

The heartfelt gift

The bond between a parent and child represents a profound connection that transcends material possessions. The greatest gift a parent can give to their children is not something tangible, but something eternal: unconditional love, sacrifice, and unwavering support. This gift is cherished, never forsaken, and carried in the heart for a lifetime.

A sacred responsibility

Children are blessings entrusted to parents for a finite time. This responsibility is sacred, like holding a delicate snowflake unique, fragile, and beautiful. Parents are called to nurture, protect, and honor their children, recognizing them as treasures beyond measure.

Agape: principled love

The essence of a parent's gift is best described by the Greek word *agape* a principled, selfless love rooted in compassion, dedication, and care. It is an unwavering commitment to guide and protect, to give freely without expectation of return. Agape compels parents to offer themselves wholly, answering the silent trust reflected in their children's eyes.

The power of love

Parental love is an enduring force. It strengthens children through hardship, instills values, and fosters resilience. Love equips them with confidence and courage, reminding them they are never alone. This legacy becomes a foundation that shapes character and inspires future generations.

The everlasting gift

Ultimately, love is the greatest inheritance. Like waves that never cease, this love is constant and unbreakable. In giving love freely, parents impart comfort, strength, and the inspiration to carry that love forward into the world.

Summation

A parent's love is a living testament, an eternal embrace, an unspoken promise, and a source of lifelong strength. Fleeting as a snowflake yet as enduring as the sea, it is a gift that transforms not only the child but the world they touch.

In It to Win It

A heartfelt letter to my eldest son

My beloved son

You are the apple of my eye. You hold the key to my heart, and your love is pure and true. Through all the challenges we have faced together, your open-heart surgery, other health struggles, and the storms of emotions and behaviors, my love for you never wavered. Having you in my life gave me the strength to heal and the courage to keep going.

My promise to you

I promise you this: I will never raise a hand to harm you. My words will always be filled with love and kindness, even when I must correct you. As your mother, it's my sacred duty to guide you, teaching you to grow into a person of character. Discipline will never mean anger or cruelty; it will mean guidance, patience, and love. I want you to grow up with integrity, compassion, and self-respect, qualities that will carry you far in life.

About your father

Although your father was not present in your everyday life, I want you to know this truth: he loves you. The last time he saw you, he made sure I knew how deeply he cared for you. I will never speak harshly of him, because I believe in the goodness within him. Like all of us, he has battles to fight and challenges to overcome before he can fully be there. But no matter the distance or time, remember that his love for you remains real and unwavering.

Forgiveness and hope

I cannot change the past, but I can promise you a brighter future. My heart is forever devoted to your happiness, your safety, and your growth. You are the greatest gift God has ever given me, and I thank Him every single day for entrusting me with you.

With all the love,

Mom

SECTION 3

Learning Love The Right Way

Learning love the right way means unlearning the habits that once confused intensity with connection. Falling too quickly and repeating toxic patterns gives way to clarity gained through a sober, honest perspective. With growth comes the ability to make better choices and recognize love rooted in respect, stability, and shared values. Marriage becomes a place where love is practiced with intention, not impulse.

Real love doesn't just feel good, it does good.

Sometimes a Boyfriend

A formal reflection on relationship expectations

Not a "now and then"

I am not intended to be anyone's "now and then." I am a person who deserves a committed partner. I cannot accept repeated excuses, especially those tied to "street business", as a reason for emotional or physical absence. Such pursuits provide no security, no fulfillment, and no lasting benefit.

An emerging pattern

It is deeply disheartening to recognize where I stand in your priorities. A clear pattern has revealed itself: in weeks when your resources are scarce and I am compensated; you return to being the caring and attentive partner I was once drawn to. But as soon as money flows into your hands, your presence fades abruptly, leaving me unsettled and searching for answers. Looking back, the cycle was always predictable. Whenever I offered support, distance soon followed. My calls unanswered, my thoughts unacknowledged, it has become clear that I am far from your mind.

Allowing exploitation

This realization forces me to confront my own vulnerability. It is painful to accept that my generosity has been met with manipulation and neglect. From this point forward, I set a firm boundary: I will not provide financial, emotional, or practical support to someone unwilling to reciprocate genuine care. Your struggles, whether hunger, hardship, or otherwise, cannot continue to be the justification for disregard.

The clear truth

The truth is now undeniable, you reach out only in times of need, and outside of those moments, my presence holds little weight in your life. I am not a convenience, nor am I a "now and then." I am worthy of recognition, respect, and sincere partnership. If you cannot acknowledge my value that I deserve, then you must accept the consequences of my departure.

Resolution and path forward

- **Self-Respect:** I will prioritize my well-being and no longer accept manipulation or undervaluing.
- **Boundaries:** I refuse to give where there is no reciprocity.
- **Strength:** I will remain anchored in my worth, knowing I deserve a partnership grounded in respect and consistency.
- **Clarity:** The pattern of this relationship is no longer hidden. If change does not occur, I will move forward without hesitation.

The reflection

This reflection is my affirmation of self-worth. I will no longer settle for conditional love, fleeting affection, or empty promises. Going forward, I choose only consistent and genuine love. I trust that my heart will recover, and by enforcing these boundaries, I prepare myself for a future defined by genuine connection, respect, and fulfillment.

I Stupidly Fell in Love

A personal reflection on vulnerability, heartbreak, and self-respect

The start

Love often arrives unexpectedly, and sometimes in ways we never anticipate. My story begins with an honest admission: I fell in love when I should have known better. What followed was a journey of discovery about me, about human nature, and about the true meaning of self-respect.

From contempt to connection

Our first meeting was anything but charming. I disliked him instantly. His unapologetic boldness and blunt honesty startled me, a sharp contrast to the sugarcoated niceties I had been accustomed to my entire life. He wasn't concerned with pleasing others, and his lack of pretense made me uncomfortable at first. Yet as our worlds collided, I found myself drawn in. Our minds began to converse deeply, and through shared thoughts of hope and happiness, love quietly began to take root.

The complexity of affection

As our relationship unfolded, I learned I was not the only woman in his life. The realization shattered me. My heart sank, and tears blurred my vision. I wanted desperately to be his one and only, to hold a special place in his life that no one else could touch. I tried everything to prove my worth why I should be his only choice. Yet, the shadows of other women lingered, always present, even when unseen. Was I special to him? Did he treat me differently than the others? These questions haunted me. If I truly mattered, there would have been no competition. But reality told me otherwise, leaving me disheartened, arm tattooed with the memory like an unwanted scar.

The sinkhole of the unknown

Why did I allow myself to fall into this emotional sinkhole? Perhaps it was the hope of finding real love, the kind that changes everything. But as I reflect now, I see the truth: I was trying to win the affection of someone not yet ready to love. I wasn't connecting with a mature man who knew what he wanted, but with a boy still searching for himself in the world.

Choosing self-respect over heartbreak

In the end, I chose to honor myself. I realized my love for me must be greater than any affection he could offer. I respect myself too much to be just a bed of convenience. To any woman in a similar place, I say this: reflect deeply. You are more than a number, more than a temporary page in someone else's story. The right man will not make you compete. He will see your worth without hesitation. We must stop grasping so tightly for love and instead allow it to find us naturally. In the meantime, we must hold fast to our dignity, our self-respect, and our self-love. Sometimes heartbreak, though painful, is the price of discovering who we truly are.

My lesson

Falling in love is never foolish. What matters is how we respond when faced with painful truths. I've learned that self-love is the foundation of a meaningful connection. I walk forward with this lesson etched into me, hopeful that my story reminds others to always choose themselves first.

Understanding the Phrase: "Get Out of Jail Ticket"

Exploring the meaning and implications in relationships

What does "get out of jail ticket" mean?

The phrase "get out of jail ticket," borrowed from Monopoly's famous "Get Out of Jail Free" card, has taken on new meaning in everyday conversation. It typically refers to an opportunity to escape consequences or avoid punishment for an action that would otherwise be unacceptable. In relationships, it can describe a one-time pass or permission to break a major rule, for example, being allowed to have a sexual encounter outside the relationship without facing repercussions.

The relationship context

I've encountered this firsthand. A friend once told her boyfriend, "You have one pass to get another piece of ass before we get married." In other words, she was granting him a one-time opportunity to be unfaithful before their wedding. While framed as a form of freedom or understanding, this idea immediately raises questions about trust, commitment, and self-worth.

Trust and boundaries in relationships

Trust is the cornerstone of every lasting relationship. When one partner feels the need to hand out a "get out of jail ticket," it may signal doubt, doubt in their partner's ability to remain faithful or in the stability of the relationship itself. On the surface, it might appear as compromise or flexibility, but beneath it often lie insecurity and fear. The reality is that giving someone permission to cheat, even once, can blur boundaries and leave wounds that are hard to heal.

Why would anyone agree to this

The reasons vary: fear of losing a partner, wanting to seem "cool" or open-minded, or believing that granting this freedom will prevent future infidelity. But these justifications rarely create healthy outcomes. Instead, they invite confusion and resentment, while setting a dangerous precedent that boundaries can be bent or broken whenever it's convenient.

Accountability and choices

If you agree to a "get out of jail ticket," you're also agreeing to the consequences that follow. When infidelity occurs, whether within the pass or beyond, you cannot ignore the role of choice. Both partners must be honest with themselves. Allowing a free pass is, in many ways, acknowledging that commitment is conditional. If betrayal later causes pain, it's important to reflect on the decision made at the start.

Self-respect and moving forward

No relationship can thrive without respect and trust. If your partner continually pushes or breaks boundaries, or if you feel pressured to allow behavior that undermines your dignity, the healthiest choice is to walk away. Real love does not require passes or loopholes. It thrives in loyalty, clarity, and mutual respect.

Final thoughts

The "get out of jail ticket" may sound like freedom, but in reality, it often opens the door to disappointment and heartbreak. Healthy relationships are built on honesty, shared values, and accountability, not on free passes that excuse betrayal. Everyone deserves consistent, respectful, and true love.

Baby Mama Drama

A father's perspective on parenting, responsibility, and relationship turmoil

Intro

This monologue aims to explore the frustration and emotional weight of a father navigating co-parenting challenges with his child's mother. It reveals the struggle to stay present and responsible while facing blame, manipulation, and conflict all while striving to put the child's well-being first.

A father's side of the story

They call me my baby's daddy, like I'm just a sperm donor, but that's not the truth. Why am I always painted as the villain? It took two of us to bring this child into the world, yet somehow, I'm the one left standing here, blamed and misunderstood. The drama didn't start with me. My child's mama brought the chaos, and her attitude is the reason I had to leave. Even after everything, I still do all I can for my child. But she holds my baby hostage, punishing me because I won't give her what she wants anymore.

The struggle for fairness

My child should never be used as a bargaining chip in this toxic game. Yet I keep hearing, "It's the baby's daddy to blame." The reality? I'm told flat out, *"If you don't sleep with me, you can't see your daughter."* Why should I have to compromise myself just to be in my child's life?

Let's be real, it was her lies, her games, her choices that brought us here. Now she's angry because I've moved on, because I refuse to tolerate her drama. She's the definition of "baby mama drama," and I had to step back to protect my peace.

Fatherhood and responsibility

I may not punch a clock at a nine-to-five, but I give my daughter what matters most, time, love, and presence. I care for her, so her mother can work. I nurture her, guide her, and make sure she knows she is loved. Yet her mother still attacks my manhood, calling me less of a man simply because I won't sleep with her anymore.

But here's the truth: being a real man isn't about giving in to her demands. It's about showing up for my child, every single day. It's about putting my daughter first, even when bitterness and pride make that harder than it should be.

The toll of conflict

This constant fighting takes its toll. Some men give up altogether because the drama feels endless. But our daughter doesn't deserve to grow up on a battlefield, caught between adult grudges. She deserves peace, stability, and love not manipulation.

One day, our daughter will see the truth for herself. She'll see who showed up and who played games. The masks will fall, and reality will speak louder than any accusations.

The revelation

This monologue shines a light on the emotional damage caused when parents weaponize their children against each other. It challenges the stereotype of the absent, careless "baby daddy" and shows another side: a father fighting to remain present, despite the obstacles.

Ultimately, the message is simple: accountability, respect, and fairness are needed on both sides. Personal pride must never come before the child's well-being. For the sake of their daughter, I pray for healing, understanding, and a future where love, not drama, guides their co-parenting journey.

Sanity Isn't Payment

Prioritizing mental well-being over toxic relationships

The price of sanity in relationships

In the pursuit of love and connection, people often find themselves entangled in relationships that are far more complicated than necessary. The truth is most of that complexity stems from our own choices and boundaries. When we're drawn to drama-filled relationships, we risk trading away our peace of mind for fleeting moments of affection. But sanity should never be for sale. Our mental well-being is more valuable than any tender gesture that comes at the cost of self-respect.

The importance of self-respect

Self-respect is the cornerstone of every healthy relationship. When we honor ourselves, it becomes easier to recognize when a situation no longer serves us. Walking away from a toxic or draining relationship is not weakness, it is courage in action. Love that demands your sanity as payment is not love at all. Choosing yourself is the greatest act of loyalty you can offer, because peace is never a fair trade for chaos.

Choosing the easier road

Life offers endless paths to joy, fulfillment, and genuine connection. Yet too often, we cling to the idea that love must come with struggle and pain. That belief is a trap. Real love doesn't need to be earned through suffering. Some relationships nurture, uplift, and create serenity. It is not only wise, but necessary to take the road that allows you to breathe freely, instead of the one that suffocates you with conflict.

Sanity should never be the price for love

Though maintaining peace of mind can sometimes feel costly, it should never become currency in the pursuit of love. Any bond that requires you to sacrifice your stability is not truly love, its control, dependency, or dysfunction in disguise. True affection strengthens your spirit, steadies your heart, and supports your sense of self. Your emotional well-being is sacred, and you deserve relationships that protect it, not deplete it.

The ultimatum

At the end of the day, the choice is yours. Decide what you're willing to sacrifice for love but let sanity be nonnegotiable. Remember, your peace is priceless. By choosing relationships that honor your mental health, you establish the standard for how you expect to be treated. Love should never come at the expense of your mind. Choose wisely and let your well-being light the way.

Reflection on Unhappiness and the Courage to Change

Understanding the roots of unhappiness and embracing hope

Why are we unhappy

Unhappiness has a way of settling into our lives sometimes quietly, other times loudly, until it feels like part of who we are. We may ask ourselves: *Why do I remain here? Why do I keep hoping things will change when they never do?* The answers aren't always clear, but the questions are a signal that it's time to face the truth.

The cycle of unhappiness

Many get stuck because of fear, self-doubt, or the false comfort of the familiar. Like a battered animal returning for food, or a woman staying in a harmful relationship because the bills are paid, we sometimes cling to what hurts us simply because it feels safe. Fear of the unknown can make misery feel like a form of security. But it isn't.

Facing fear and breaking free

There is no reason to stay in pain. Deep down, most of us know this truth: people will treat us the way we allow them to. When we tolerate mistreatment, it continues. That is why self-love and clear boundaries are not luxuries; they are survival tools.

The strength to change

Change is not easy. It takes courage to shake off what's familiar and step into the unknown. But it is possible and worth it. The first steps may feel heavy, but over time, they get lighter. Choosing happiness over unhappiness is an act of bravery, and the reward is peace.

Embracing happiness

If you are trapped in unhappiness, remember you are not powerless. Muster the strength, trust your worth, and take one step forward. Change may be uncomfortable but staying stuck costs far more. True happiness begins the moment you believe you deserve it and refuse to settle for less.

Self-Respect and Integrity in Relationships

Upholding individuality and mutual value

Frustration often arises in relationships when acts of kindness, loyalty, or integrity go unnoticed or are taken for granted. The key to rising above this is maintaining a strong sense of self-worth. When you refuse to let others define you, you build the foundation for healthier and more balanced connections.

The impact of unfair comparisons

One of the most damaging habits in relationships is comparison measuring one person against another. These unfair comparisons diminish individuality and cloud the value someone truly brings. Honesty, loyalty, and respect deserve to be recognized on their own merit, not overshadowed by past disappointments or the failures of others.

Genuine affection versus insincerity

True affection cannot be faked. It stands apart from shallow gestures and insincere games. Those who are grounded in self-respect refuse to let external judgments or insecurities diminish them of their worth. This clarity allows space for love that is genuine, consistent, and uplifting.

Embracing individuality for meaningful connections

Moving past old wounds and honoring each person's individuality opens the door to authentic, respectful, and lasting relationships. When both people are seen, heard, and valued for who they truly are, the relationship becomes not just sustainable but transformative.

Gratefulness: A Reflection on Appreciation

Understanding and expressing true gratitude

What it means to be grateful

Gratefulness is more than a fleeting feeling or polite gesture; it is a powerful state of appreciation that shapes how we see the world and the people in it. To be grateful is to recognize the blessings, support, and love we receive in the most unexpected ways. Amid life's uncertainties, gratefulness allows us to see people and moments as gifts that enrich our journey.

True gratitude blends joy and humility. It's about honoring the presence of those who quietly become part of our lives, making them richer and more meaningful without disruption or demand.

Grateful to you: A personal tribute

I am deeply grateful for you, not just for your companionship, but for the way you've woven yourself into my life. Your arrival didn't turn my world upside down; instead, it brought comfort, stability, and inspiration that I had been searching for. You are irreplaceable, a blessing I would never want to lose.

In my moments of prayer and reflection, I thank God for you first. Your presence feels like an unexpected gift, wrapped in mystery but filled with meaning. Since you entered my life, my gratitude for you has only deepened, untouchable by anyone or anything else.

The gift of gratefulness

True gratefulness transforms us. It compels us to notice the extraordinary in the ordinary, to honor those who uplift us, and to express our appreciation openly and wholeheartedly. Gratitude is not just a feeling; it's an action, making sure the people we treasure know how deeply they matter.

For me, gratefulness is embodied in our relationship. It is a celebration not only of who you are, but of the ways you've shaped my life for the better.

The realization

Gratefulness is a force that binds hearts and nurtures relationships. To live with gratitude is to live with intention, to see the blessings before us, and to make sure the ones we value know the depth of our appreciation. For you, my gratitude knows no bounds, and I am deeply honored to share my life with a person like you.

SECTION 4

The Workplace as a Mirror: Discovery and Growth

The workplace becomes a mirror, reflecting both self-discovery and growth under pressure. Experiences with arrogance, corporate racism, and undermining leadership reveal how power can either erode or elevate human dignity. Communication breakdowns and generational clashes challenge understanding and adaptability, while education used as a tool for division exposes deeper inequities. In these spaces, character—not credentials or status—defines true integrity and progress.

True worth is not measured by titles, degrees, or status but by character.

Racism in the Corporate Space of Small Businesses

Pitfalls, behaviors, and what truly matters watching it as it unfolded (2001)

Racism is not confined to large corporations with complex hierarchies and policies. It also surfaces in smaller, privately owned businesses, where the attitudes and culture are shaped by the choices of a single leader. When those in charge allow personal bias to guide decisions, the entire workplace reflects it.

When personal bias sets the tone

In small businesses, the owner's perspective often becomes the company standard. If racial bias is ignored, excused, or minimized, employees quickly learn that speaking up is risky and silence is safer. Subtle comments, jokes, or exclusions may seem insignificant to outsiders, but to those experiencing them, they reinforce inequality and erode trust.

The danger of dismissal

One of the most significant pitfalls is brushing off discriminatory behavior as unimportant, dismissing it as personality quirks or "just how things are done." Over time, these unchecked actions create a culture where fairness is optional, and respect is conditional. The damage doesn't stop at individuals; it weakens the organization, fueling turnover and discouraging loyalty.

Beyond surface values

Owners may talk about fairness and equity, but values are proven through practices, not words. Every hiring decision, every promotion, and every interaction is an opportunity to either reinforce integrity or reveal hypocrisy. True equity requires consistency, not convenience.

What really matters

A business functions best when every employee feels respected and valued. Success depends not on who holds power but on whether that power is exercised with fairness and accountability. Small businesses, perhaps more than large ones, need to pay close attention to the everyday choices that define culture.

My perspective

In 2001, I witnessed firsthand how quickly bias could shape the environment of a smaller company. It wasn't always loud or obvious, but it showed up in who was listened to, who was dismissed, and who was left out. The lesson was clear: racism in the workplace doesn't always roar; it often whispers, but its effects are just as damaging.

Can't Get Me to Listen

A reflection on respect and communication in a hostile work environment (2006)

Context

In 2006, I found myself in a hostile workplace where shouting replaced dialogue and respect was scarce. To process the experience, I wrote a poem that used animalistic imagery, biting, gnawing, and pouncing, to capture how aggression in the workplace can strip people of their dignity.

Reflection

When leaders attack with words instead of guiding with clarity, the effect is dehumanizing. Aggression may force compliance in the moment, but it breeds fear, resentment, and a culture of silence. It feels less like collaboration and more like survival, dodging claws rather than sharing ideas.

The golden rule applies as much in business as in life: *treat others as you would want to be treated.* Respect can't be demanded through force; it must be earned through fairness, empathy, and humility. A sharp tone or public rebuke may leave scars, but kindness and patience build trust that lasts.

The value of kindness

Kindness costs little but creates space where people feel safe to contribute. Honey attracts bees far more than vinegar ever will. In any workplace, positive reinforcement opens doors, while hostility only closes them.

The call for respect

Respect is the proper foundation of effective communication. To be heard, one must also listen. To inspire effort, one must treat others as human beings, not as prey. That was the truth behind my words in 2006, and it's a truth that matters even today.

Respect Beyond Resumes

Why every worker's contribution fuels workplace success

Intelligence and communication in the workplace

Intelligence and communication matter in any professional setting, but they should never be used to make others feel less important. Advanced vocabulary or formal education may signal expertise, but they are not the sole markers of wisdom or capability. True value lies in how knowledge is applied—with clarity, respect, and the ability to bring others along.

Every voice matters

Workplaces thrive when ideas are communicated in ways that encourage collaboration and mutual respect. The best leaders and colleagues use language to connect rather than exclude, creating an environment where all perspectives are welcomed and heard.

Brains, hands, and heart

A successful organization depends on more than degrees or titles. Brains, hands, and heart all play critical roles—from strategy and decision-making to the hands-on work that keeps operations moving. Each contribution matters, and success comes when all skills are recognized as essential to the whole.

The takeaway

Respect beyond resumes means acknowledging that intelligence comes in many forms. Businesses grow stronger when they value both education and lived experience, fostering cultures where everyone's contribution is seen, respected, and essential to success.

Workplace Communication and Generational Dynamics

The evolution of business culture

The importance of communication in business culture

Business culture is constantly evolving, and open, honest communication has become more important than ever. Creating an environment free from distractions, biases, and hidden agendas fosters trust and collaboration. Clear communication not only strengthens relationships between colleagues but also ensures those connections are grounded in respect and integrity. It remains one of the most valuable assets a team can have, helping them navigate challenges and seize opportunities with confidence.

Promoting open dialogue

Modern workplaces emphasize cultures where questions are welcomed, and discussions happen without fear of judgment. When done well, this approach nurtures collaboration, learning, and growth. Still, consistency is not always easy, even in organizations that value openness. Everyday choices in word, tone, and behavior can either encourage or discourage dialogue. With intention, however, communication becomes the foundation for professional development and stronger team dynamics.

Generational perspectives in the workplace

Generational diversity brings both challenges and opportunities. Gen Z, having grown up in a digital-first world, often shows fluency in technology, social media, and awareness of social justice and political issues. Research suggests they bring high emotional intelligence and a natural inclination toward activism qualities that can strengthen organizational culture. Older generations, by contrast, often lean on resilience, patience, and lived experience. Together, these strengths create a balance between innovation and perspective, helping teams thrive in a changing world.

Challenges in bridging generations

At times, differences in approach can feel like friction, one group moves quickly, the other prefers a steady pace; one prizes new ideas, the other values lessons already learned. Yet these contrasts don't have to divide us. With empathy and curiosity, they become opportunities to learn from one another, creating teams that are both grounded and forward-thinking.

Future challenges and opportunities

Looking ahead, workplaces need to balance the enthusiasm of fresh talent with the wisdom of experience. Hiring practices that value only one side risk missing the benefits of the other. By ensuring that both education and lived experience are respected, organizations can build stronger, more sustainable teams that bridge divides and carry business culture forward with integrity and vision.

SECTION 5

Finding Self-Worth Beyond Society's Mirror

Finding self-worth beyond society's mirror requires rejecting false measures of success and the pressure of "have vs. have not" thinking. It means confronting distorted beliefs about money, moving from survival and dependence toward responsibility and self-respect. Through self-care, freedom replaces comparison, and clarity replaces performance. Letting go of social media illusions makes space for authenticity and grounded confidence.

Society cannot define my value, only I can.

Braggarts: From Personal Experience

Understanding the need to boast and its impact on others

This was my 25-year-old self

At 25, I often asked myself: *Why do people who already have so much feel the need to brag to those who have less?* There's a difference between sharing happiness and rubbing it in. Sharing is about inviting others into your joy; bragging is about making yourself feel taller by making others feel smaller.

Scripture reminds us to *"rejoice with those who rejoice and mourn with those who mourn."* That's the spirit of connection, lifting each other in good times and standing together in hard times. Sharing brings people closer. Boasting, on the other hand, creates distance.

Too often, what I heard wasn't celebration, it was competition. The new car, the big vacation, the money spent, it wasn't being shared with me; it was being flaunted at me. And all it did was highlight what I didn't have.

My own reality at the time? My "big trip" was to McDonald's for a supersized fry. Not glamorous, but it was mine, and I enjoyed it. That little joy mattered to me, just as their joy mattered to them. The difference was, I didn't need to make someone else feel less to appreciate it.

Why do people brag?

A therapist once explained that bragging often comes from insecurity, a need for attention, or even just a habit. But when it crosses the line into belittling others, it stops being about joy and becomes about control. The subtext isn't "I'm happy," it's "I'm better than you."

The impact on others

Hearing that kind of boasting can sting, especially when you're struggling. It can turn conversations into contests, leaving one person feeling small and unseen. Over time, that arrogance poisons relationships.

Empathy and consideration

There's nothing wrong with sharing good news, but the way it's shared matters. If it uplifts and invites others in, it creates a connection. If it diminishes or excludes, it becomes arrogance. The real connections are built not through comparison, but through compassion, when we honor scripture's wisdom: *rejoice together in victories and stand together in struggles.*

Final Thought

Real wealth is not about possessions or titles, but humility, gratitude, and the ability to share joy without making others feel less than.

A Beggar's Recovery

From desperation to determination: One Stranger's Journey

Street life isn't romantic

Life on the streets is rarely romanticized by those who have truly lived it. Homelessness and addiction are not adventures; they are daily battles marked by hunger, judgment, and survival. I know this firsthand, having been both a beggar and a struggling single parent, wearing two very different but equally heavy hats.

Harsh realities

Every day, the familiar sight of strangers asking for spare change can wear thin. I've thought to myself, *"I get tired of seeing your face, always asking me to spare a dime or two."* And yet, I've been on the other side of that exchange. As a single parent, every dollar mattered. It could mean food for my child or nothing at all.

And as someone who once begged, I knew the stigma: the assumption that the money would be spent on drugs or alcohol. That belief isn't always wrong. I admit it freely: *"I chose to use drugs. I chose to sniff coke up my nose."* It was my reality, and my downfall.

My Turning Point

Eventually, bitterness gave way to truth. One day, I realized: *"I'm tired of looking for handouts without putting forth effort. I'd rather earn my keep, proud that I put out the labor and got paid."*

That moment was my turning point; the day I chose self-respect over dependency. It was the beginning of recovery. I decided to clean up my life, not only for myself but to prove that transformation is possible. My message is simple and clear: *"You can too. It is never too late."* Defeat begins in the mind, and so does determination.

A message to the beggar and to all of us

When I stopped giving money to those who begged, it wasn't from cruelty. It was from hard-earned wisdom. *"Stop asking me for money that I worked hard for. Stop expecting me to steal from my child's mouth to feed you."*

What I offer instead is encouragement: seek dignity through effort, not pity. Walk away from dependency. Choose to earn, not to expect.

Final thought

This story isn't just about a beggar's recovery; it's about the power of responsibility, the necessity of choice, and the hope that anyone, no matter how far gone, can still stand up and start again.

The hands that once begged now work. The voice that once pleaded for pity now speaks with strength. The spirit that once felt broken now stands tall, building a future with determination.

Media-Formed Lies

A realization of deception, influence, and awareness

The manipulation of fear

The media have long understood the power of fear. It is made available to anyone who has the ability to twist words, bend truths, and bombard ears until confusion sets in. What begins as "information" often disguises itself as entertainment or urgency, leaving innocent people caught in its web of distortion.

When lies feel like truth

The danger lies in repetition. When the same messages are spoken over and over, they begin to sound believable, even when rooted in deceit. Too often, we rely on voices that do not have our best interests at heart. In doing so, we compromise our own clarity, becoming entangled in narratives that serve profit, not truth.

The violence of words

Words can wound as deeply as actions. Headlines slash at emotions, stories twist reality, and entire groups are defamed easily. Lies are sold without hesitation, and many innocent souls pay the price. These deceptions thrive not in truth but in the chaos; they plant fear and mistrust in the hearts of those who listen.

The cost of apathy

The most dangerous response to manipulation is apathy. To sit aloof, ignoring distortion, is to allow lies to fester unchecked. When we let "garbage tickle our ears," we surrender our judgment to those who profit from division and destruction. Silence becomes complicity.

The realization

The media is not always the friend it pretends to be. It can rush in like an intruder, cloaked in authority, yet driven by profit and power. The realization is sobering: to protect ourselves, we must question, discern, and think critically. Truth cannot be consumed blindly; it must be sought with intention.

Societal Box

A reflection on freedom, control, and self-liberation

Beyond the box

Life is not meant to be confined. It moves like a current, sometimes fast, sometimes slow, and each of us must decide whether to flow with it or remain trapped within the boundaries set for us. Connection is part of that flow. You and I are not separate; our collective voices, joy, and struggles all rise together to bring color and meaning to the world.

Breaking free from illusions

Too often, reality is shaped by outside forces, television, media, and the constant stream of cultural expectations. These influences sell distraction as truth and conformity as success. Many accept this without question, living inside a societal box built for them. But freedom begins when you choose to question, to see beyond the illusions, and to claim your own perspective.

Refusing control

You cannot live authentically if you allow yourself to be controlled. The world will always try to slow you down with noise, comparison, and manipulation. But the choice is yours: remain distracted or keep moving forward. When you refuse to play the societal games, you reclaim your power to define your own path.

Choosing knowledge over chains

Superficial measures of worth, money, image, and status are poor substitutes for truth. They keep people bound in invisible chains, always striving but never fulfilled. Knowledge is what cuts those chains. Awareness creates freedom. When you choose understanding over appearance, you gain clarity, and with clarity comes power.

The realization

True liberation begins in the mind. It's not about escaping society but about refusing to be controlled by its illusions. To live freely, you must choose awareness over distraction, knowledge over manipulation, and authenticity over conformity. In that choice, you step outside the box and into your own freedom.

Mystical Mind

A reflection on freedom, knowledge, and self-realization

Thinking beyond the limits

A mystical mind resists confinement. It refuses to succumb to the narrow boundaries set by society or allow fear to dictate its path. Instead, it seeks knowledge wherever it can be found, knowing that wisdom is the highest form of power. When you commit to learning and expanding your perspective, you strengthen your place in the world and realize your own potential.

Living for truth, not approval

A mystical mind can differentiate between living authentically and living for validation. It does not waste time trying to impress others. Instead, it draws energy from curiosity, imagination, and love for life itself. By valuing truth over performance, you refuse to wear masks or conform and instead move through life with purpose and clarity.

Life on your terms

Life is not defined by what is handed to you, but by what you make out of it. A mystical mind treats challenges as opportunities and dreams as starting points, not fantasies. Living on your terms means refusing to settle for the easy road of conformity and instead shaping reality with conscious decisions rooted in freedom and curiosity.

The vantage point

A mystical mind is not simply something you're born with; it's a choice you make every day. It's the decision to keep learning, to live authentically, and to see beyond the limits others accept. In choosing this path, you realize a deeper truth: the only real boundaries you face are the ones you allow.

The Hard Road: Why Are You Taking It?

Words for my sons and young men labeled "worthless," but full of worth

Life isn't always what it seems

From the outside, your life may look reckless and hard. From the outside, mine may look easy. But appearances deceive. The truth is, both lives carry struggle. Every day I fight to keep ignorance, negativity, and chaos from pulling me off course. And here's what I want you to know: you are far more valuable than you've been told. Others may not see it yet, but that doesn't change the fact that it's true.

Drama is not strength

Living in constant chaos is exhausting, not empowering. Strength isn't found in fights, conflict, or fear; it's found in control. Always looking over your shoulder, always waiting for the next confrontation, isn't living. Ending up in an early grave because of choices within your control is not destiny; it's called surrender. Ask yourself: Am I chasing a rush, an image, or something deeper? When you strip it all back, what remains? That answer is who you really are.

Potential is your real power

Inside you, there is more potential than the streets could ever offer. The world may not reflect it to you yet, but that doesn't mean it's not there. Respect doesn't come from intimidation; it comes from discipline, character, and consistency. You don't need to wear toughness like armor. Real strength is walking away from what diminishes you. Real courage is becoming who you're meant to be, not who others expect you to be.

A future worth building

Your life is too precious to waste. It is worth more than violence, pride, more than a casket and your mother's tears. There is a bigger world waiting for you, closer than you realize. When I look at you, I don't see "worthless." I see resilience. I see strength. I see potential. Don't let the lies you've been told dictate your story. Don't let the streets write your ending.

In the end

You are not worthless, you are unfinished. Every day you wake up, you're given a new chance to choose differently. To rise. To grow. To live on your own terms. Your belief in yourself will be the bridge between who you are today and the man you'll become.

SECTION 6

The Human Side of Life and Politics

The human side of life and politics is rooted in empathy, reflection, and shared responsibility. Honest reflections on racial healing and human connection invite understanding beyond division. Rediscovering common sense as lived wisdom shifts focus from rhetoric to action, reminding us that progress begins in everyday choices and relationships.

Real change begins at home, with wisdom that is lived, not just spoken.

Racism Justified

A reflection on skewed perception, false validation, and God's truth

The distorted perception

For centuries, societies operated under the lie that being Black was somehow wrong, a flaw in God's creation. Skin color became the basis for mistreatment, exclusion, and violence. What should have been recognized as part of the beauty and diversity of humanity was twisted into something "less than." The worth of an entire people was questioned, not because of anything they had done, but simply because of who they were.

The misuse of scripture

To make matters worse, oppressors often turned to scripture as a tool of control. They justified slavery, segregation, and brutality by lifting words out of context and bending them to fit their own agenda. Holding a Bible in one hand while stripping dignity with the other, they claimed righteousness while sinning. But scripture was never meant to justify hate. God is love, and His creation reflects that love. To deny the humanity of one group is to reject God Himself.

The truth of God's creation

At the time of creation, God did not ask permission from man to determine who should exist and in what form. Each life was intentionally made, each person bearing the image of God. Race, skin color, and culture were never mistakes; they were expressions of divine design. Any ideology that seeks to demean, divide, or destroy people based on race stands in direct opposition to the Creator's intent.

The consequences of false justification

The false narrative that Blackness was inferior inflicted generational wounds. Families were torn apart, opportunities stolen, lives cut short. And still, those responsible attempted to cover their actions with religion, using the very Word of God against His people. Yet, history has shown that such false justification could never erase truth. The resilience of the oppressed, their faith, and their refusal to be defined by lies are living proof that God's image cannot be diminished.

The ultimate reality

In the end, no scripture can erase the truth: God is love, and His love extends to all of His creation. There is no hierarchy of worth in His design. Any attempt to justify racism by using the Bible is not only misguided but blasphemous; it denies the very heart of God. Humanity was created for coexistence, unity, dignity, and love. Racism was never justified, and it never will be.

Standing Together

A reflection on unity, peace, and shared responsibility

A vision of unity

At our core, we are not separate; we are connected. What happens to one of us affects all of us. When we stand together, we shine brighter than any single individual can on their own. Unity is not just an ideal; it is a practical path forward. It's how communities grow stronger, how nations heal, and how we build a future where peace is possible.

Moving beyond fear and division

Too often, fear keeps us divided. We fear what we don't understand, and we hesitate to imagine a world where conflict and disunity are not the norm. But peace is not weakness, and unity is not naive. Coming together across differences requires courage, not passivity. Real strength comes from listening, understanding, and recognizing that what we share as human beings is far greater than what divides us.

Working with, not against

For true unity to last, people and governments must work together. Division between the two only creates distrust and stagnation. Governments should reflect the people's hopes, not amplify their fears. And people must take responsibility too by engaging, by holding leaders accountable, and by choosing collaboration over conflict. Progress is only possible when both sides walk the path together.

Choosing love and respect

The foundation of peace is respect. When we love ourselves, we become capable of loving others. When we honor one another's humanity, war, violence, and inequality lose their power. Unity is not abstract; it shows up in everyday choices: how we treat neighbors, how we listen to those we disagree with, and how we act when faced with injustice.

The realization

The future is not written for us; it is created by us. Division will only weaken us, but unity can transform us. If people and governments commit to working hand in hand, there is no limit to what can be achieved. The world does not need more conflict; it needs cooperation. Peace is not a dream; it is a decision.

Our Voices Were Heard in a Dream

A reflection on unity, education, and equal opportunity

A shared vision

Imagine sitting together in one room, recognizing that we represent the entire world. We breathe the same air, we carry the same hopes, and we long for a life free from despair. Now picture a world where differences in color, culture, or creed are not barriers but strengths, where people unite around shared dreams of peace, progress, and opportunity.

Education is the key

One of the most important of those dreams is education. Knowledge is the foundation that allows us to overcome obstacles once thought impossible. It opens doors that poverty, prejudice, or fear once kept closed. But this dream should not come at the cost of lifelong debt. Higher education must be obtainable for all, without financial chains that punish those simply seeking to learn and grow.

Moving beyond false promises

For too long, many have been lured by promises of prosperity through other means, only to find themselves paying the highest price. Unlike those hollow assurances, education offers real advancement, lasting pride, and a future that doesn't require sacrifice in vain. It is the one investment no one can take away from you, but only if society ensures it does not require crushing debt as the entry fee.

A collective responsibility

Your success is not only for yourself, but it also inspires your family, your community, and future generations. Life rewards the discipline, time, and sacrifices you put into learning. The more we unite in pursuing education for all, the stronger, more just, and more resilient our societies become.

The outlook

Knowledge is power. When education is truly accessible, without the burden of debt, we move closer to a world of peace, equality, and shared prosperity. Education is not a privilege, it is humanity's greatest equalizer, and it belongs to us all.

SECTION 7

Walking Away Stronger

Walking away stronger means embracing every challenge as an opportunity to grow. Lessons from recovery, love, parenthood, relationships, work, society, and faith converge, shaping resilience, wisdom, and purpose. Each setback becomes a teacher, each victory a testament to perseverance.

Every struggle became my teacher; every lesson became my strength.

Finding Strength Through Life's Experiences

Embracing our differences and pursuing growth

Life as a teacher

Life unfolds as a journey filled with challenges, victories, and defining moments that test who we truly are. Each experience, whether uplifting or challenging, shapes our identity and fuels our growth. Through them, we uncover inner strength, resilience, and wisdom that no book or speech alone can provide.

The power of embracing uniqueness

One of the most profound realizations we can embrace is the uniqueness of every individual. Our backgrounds, perspectives, and aspirations set us apart, yet we are united in our pursuit of meaning and happiness. By welcoming these differences, we create opportunities to learn from one another, fostering empathy, respect, and unity. Though our paths may differ, our journeys are connected.

Lessons from the streets of life

The streets, both literal and symbolic, teach lessons that can't be learned in classrooms. Conversations with strangers, facing obstacles head-on, or witnessing unexpected acts of kindness all shape our perspective. These experiences cultivate adaptability, compassion, and resourcefulness. Even in adversity, life offers lessons that can strengthen and transform us if we remain open to them.

Staying true to your path

Staying grounded in your values and focused on your aspirations is essential. There will always be critics, doubters, and distractions. Don't let them deter you. Let their words push you forward, reminding you of your potential. Your worth is not defined by their perception but by your persistence and commitment to your goals.

Building a meaningful life

Fulfillment doesn't come from perfection; it comes from courage, authenticity, and resilience. By embracing experiences, respecting differences, and continuing to grow, you turn life's challenges into steppingstones. Each lesson learned and each obstacle overcome moves you closer to becoming the best version of yourself.

You Can Shine

A reflection on resilience, purpose, and authentic success

Defining your own success

Your success in life is determined by the effort you invest in your goals. If you do nothing, don't expect anything in return. The world can be restless and unforgiving, but your strength and persistence matter. Never let your hard work be wasted, celebrate the fruits of your labor, and don't feel obligated to share it with those who haven't contributed or supported you.

Guarding your circle

You are only as good as you allow yourself to be. Don't let critics, doubters, or leeches drain your energy or ride on the qualities that make you shine in a fogged-out world. Surround yourself with people who share your values and your drive. Anyone who hasn't proven themselves worthy of your trust should not occupy your life, your home, or your heart.

Staying grounded

True success is not built on shortcuts or quick fixes. It comes from patience, faith, and integrity. Only by God's grace, and by trusting Him, will you find the strength to keep moving forward.

Staying on track

You have one life. Use it wisely. Stay focused, stay faithful, and stay resilient. Don't dim your light for anyone; shine bright, shine free, and let your life be the proof that you were made for more.

I'm Not Convinced

A reflection on self-discovery and what it really means to be "real"

Redefining "real"

Many people claim to be "real," but often what they mean is staying stuck in a limited version of life. Selling drugs, hustling for survival, or tearing others down isn't authenticity; it's confinement. True realism isn't about repeating cycles; it's about-facing life honestly and striving to break through them.

The trap of narrow thinking

When we define reality, only by the environment we grew up in, we miss the bigger picture. Calling hardship "real" doesn't make it the whole truth. It simply reflects a narrow vision shaped by circumstance, not possibility. If your reality is only what surrounds you, then you're not living freely; you're trapped by what others want you to believe.

The essence of being real

Being real is about self-education, growth, and the courage to see beyond what you've been told you are. It means showing compassion, uplifting others, and contributing to something greater than yourself. It's about living with integrity, choosing purpose over destruction, and truth over illusions.

Food for thought

Reality is not what you're given; it's what you create out of it. To be someone who faces struggles head-on, you need to learn from it and build a life that reflects strength, wisdom, and growth. Authenticity isn't about survival in the box; it's about breaking the box entirely.

Circles

Life moves in circles; what goes around comes around. Each turn brings lessons, growth, and new perspectives. In time, you meet a wiser, stronger version of yourself, standing in a better place than where you began.

Thank you for walking this journey with me and embracing **Street Therapy:** *A Dose of Reality*. May these words remind you that growth is always possible, healing is always within reach, and your circle will always lead you back to your true self.

With gratitude and respect, many blessings and abundant success in your journey through life.

www.ingramcontent.com/pod-product-compliance
Lightning Source LLC
LaVergne TN
LVHW080531210926
848481LV00021B/2480
* 9 7 9 8 8 9 1 7 0 6 7 8 1 *